THINGS
WITH
WINGS

Bats
Nature's Night Flyers

Frankie Stout

PowerKiDS press.

New York

To the many cool Chiroptera I have known

Published in 2009 by The Rosen Publishing Group, Inc.
29 East 21st Street, New York, NY 10010

First Edition

Editor: Nicole Pristash
Book Design: Kate Laczynski
Photo Researcher: Jessica Gerweck

Photo Credits: Cover, p. 1 © Michael Dumam/Getty Images, Inc.; p. 5 © Kevin Smith/www.istockphoto.com; p. 7 © Hugo Willcox/Getty Images, Inc.; pp. 9, 21 © Superstock.com; pp. 11, 15, 19 Shutterstock.com; p. 13 © Hazlan Abdul Hakim/www.istockphoto.com; p. 17 © Mark Moffett/Getty Images, Inc.

Library of Congress Cataloging-in-Publication Data

Stout, Frankie.
  Bats : nature's night flyers / Frankie Stout. — 1st ed.
      p. cm. — (Things with wings)
  Includes index.
  ISBN 978-1-4042-4496-2 (library binding)
  1. Bats—Juvenile literature. I. Title.
  QL737.C5S747 2009
  599.4—dc22
                                          2008006800

Manufactured in the United States of America

CONTENTS

Bats Are Things with Wings

Have you ever seen a dark animal flying over your head at night? That animal may have been a bat! Bats come out at night to hunt, eat, and fly around.

Bats are a very special type of **mammal**. They are the only type of mammal that has wings. Bats are cool because other mammals cannot fly, and bats can.

Bats can also do things other animals with wings cannot do, such as use their own sounds to find food. There are many other interesting facts about bats, so there is a lot to learn!

There are more than 950 types of bats on Earth. Bats live in every part of the world except Antarctica.

The Furriest Flyers

A bat's body is very furry. A bat's fur can be black, brown, gray, or even red. Some people think bats look like mice with wings. However, not all bats are as small as mice. Some bats have wingspans of more than 6 feet (2 m). The wingspan is the length of a bat's wings, from one tip to the other tip.

Small bats are called microbats. They have round heads, which can have many folds. They have these folds because microbats use their entire heads like ears. Other bats have larger bodies, long faces, and large eyes. These bigger bats are called megabats.

This is a little brown bat, which is a microbat. The little brown bat is the most common type of bat found in the United States.

Bat Wings

A bat's wings are special because they do not have feathers. Instead, a bat's wings are made of skin, which goes over the bat's arms, hands, and fingers. A bat's fingers are very long, and they can bend easily without breaking.

Bats use their wings for hunting, eating, and flying. A bat can catch food to eat with its wings. It can then use its wings to hold on to its food while it eats, too. Bats can also use their wings to **steer** as they fly. Their wings have special hairs that help bats find their way through the air.

This flying fox bat has very large wings. Its wings help it do important things, such as fly in a certain direction and hang on to fruit when it eats.

To the Bat Cave!

Bats are found all over the world. They live in barns, caves, and in trees. In cities, bats roost under bridges, and they can even get into people's attics. Even though bats are most at home in the wild, they can **adapt** to living in many places.

Bats are **nocturnal**, so they like to sleep during the day. Bats look for dark, safe places to rest. By hiding during the day and sleeping, bats can stay safe from **predators**. A cave is a good place for a bat to live. Bats also do well in forests, where they can live with many other bats.

A cave is a good place for a bat to stay warm in the winter and to gather with other bats. These bats are sleeping in their cave.

The Lives of Bats

Many types of bats are **social**. Whether in the wild or in cities, social bats like to stick together. This means they spend their time in groups, called colonies. These bats sleep together in groups to stay warm. In fact, many bats sleep upside down! A bat will hold on to the side of a cave or the branch of a tree with its claws.

Some people think that bats are scary because of how they look and because they bite. A few kinds of bats feed on the blood of animals, but most bats do not bother people.

These bats have wrapped their wings around their bodies. This helps the bats sleep. It also helps keep them safe, because some predators think the bats are dead leaves.

Night Feeders

Bats like to feed at night. Microbats, or smaller bats, generally eat bugs. Large megabats, however, eat mostly fruit, or they feed on flower **nectar**.

To hunt, microbats use echolocation. Echolocation means that when a microbat makes a sound, this sound **bounces** off other things, like trees and bugs. This lets the bat know where its food is. Echolocation is to bats what hearing is to people.

Megabats, though, use their noses and eyes to hunt. Some people think that all bats see poorly, but this is not true of megabats. Megabats can see well, even at night.

The Egyptian fruit bat eats large amounts of fruit every night. This bat generally likes soft fruit because it is easy to eat.

15

Who Eats Bats?

Because they are good flyers, bats can be hard for a predator to catch. However, other flying animals, like owls and even other bats, feed on bats. Sometimes, a bat will roost low, near the ground, for a short time. This is when a ground animal, such as a raccoon or a cat, gets its chance to catch a bat and eat it.

One animal, known as the bat hawk, eats bats as well. Bat hawks are birds that live in Africa and Asia. Bat hawks may eat birds and bugs, too, but they are known for eating mostly bats.

Here you can see a tarantula feeding on a bat. These large spiders can feed on bats that roost in trees or on bats that have fallen to the ground.

Pups and Mothers

Bats hunt and eat, but they also breed. Breeding is the way animals make babies. Baby bats are called pups. A bat mother generally has one pup. However, sometimes a mother bat can have twins.

Bat pups are very small. They need their mothers to feed them and keep them warm. Since a pup cannot fly when it is born, it will hang on to its mother as she flies. A pup first drinks milk from its mother. After two to four months, the pup learns how to fly by itself. Then, the pup learns to feed itself by catching bugs or finding fruit.

This bat pup is holding on to its mother's fur. Soon, the pup will be too big for its mother to carry. The pup will then start to learn how to fly on its own.

The Flying Fox

Flying fox bats are the largest bats in the world. They live in East Africa, Asia, Australia, and the islands of the Pacific Ocean. The large flying fox, or *Pteropus vampyrus*, can weigh up to 3 ½ pounds (2 kg). The wingspan of a large flying fox can be more than 6 feet (2 m)!

Flying foxes are also called fruit bats. This is because they eat mostly fruit. A flying fox will even **squeeze** a piece of fruit in its mouth until it gets all the juice out. Then the bat will spit out the rest!

This man is holding a black flying fox bat. This bat is the largest kind of bat in Australia.

It's a Bat's World

Bats are often misunderstood. Many people believe **myths** that are told about bats. For example, some people think bats like to fly in your hair or drink your blood. This is not true.

Bats are an important part of our **ecosystem**. Some bats eat bugs, which keeps the number of bugs down. Other bats help plants by taking **pollen** with them from flower to flower. Flowers need this pollen to make seeds.

Bats do good things. The next time you see a bat flying over your head at night, do not be scared. Remember all the good things bats do for our Earth!

adapt (uh-DAPT) To change to fit requirements.

bounces (BOWNS-ez) Springs up, down, or to the side.

ecosystem (EE-koh-sis-tem) A community of living things and the place in which they live.

mammal (MA-mul) A warm-blooded animal that has a backbone and hair, breathes air, and feeds milk to its young.

myths (MITHS) Stories that people make up to explain things that happen.

nectar (NEK-tur) Sweet matter found in flowers.

nocturnal (nok-TUR-nul) Active during the night.

pollen (PAH-lin) A yellow dust made by the male parts of flowers.

predators (PREH-duh-terz) Animals that kill other animals for food.

social (SOH-shul) Living together in a group.

squeeze (SKWEEZ) To force together.

steer (STEER) To make turns.

INDEX

WEB SITES

Due to the changing nature of Internet links, PowerKids Press has developed an online list of Web sites related to the subject of this book. This site is updated regularly. Please use this link to access the list:
www.powerkidslinks.com/wings/bats/

24